# The New
# Twinkle
# Twinkle

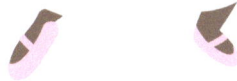

By Steve & Melissa Joseph

Illustrated by Anna Yoong

Published by: Wendiilou Publishing
Wendy Brown

Cover and book design: Anna Yoong

For more copies, contact the publisher c/-
212 Glenburnie Road
Rob Roy NSW 2360
wendiiloupublishing@gmail.com
0468 998 268
www.wendiilou.com.au

## For Mia
Our first precious child. You are so loved.

## For Maya
Beautiful, just the way you are.

Twinkle twinkle, you're a star

*Made in His image*

That's who you are

Loved, *unique*

and one of a kind

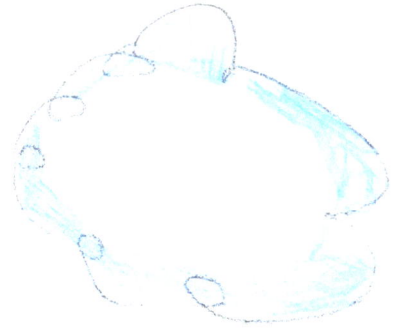

Before the world began

He had you in mind

Twinkle, twinkle

You're a star

*Made in His image*

That's who you are

Knit together *perfectly*

"I am fearfully and wonderfully made."

- Psalm 139 -

Image of Christ on

you permanently

Not defined by the
world that you see

You knit me
together in my
mother's womb.

I am fearfully
and wonderfully
made.

*Be defined* by the

Word that you read

You're a child of the King

That's *royalty*

Loved by Him...

...immeasurably!

The apple of His eye
*His celebration*

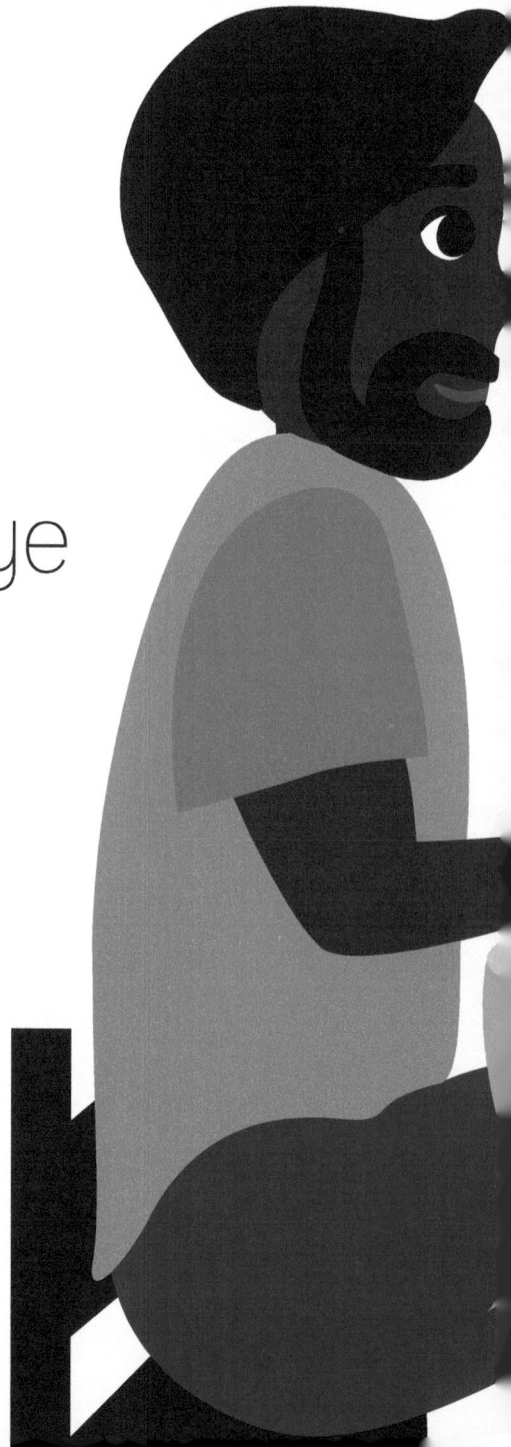

*Be joyful,*

joyful in His salvation

www.ingramcontent.com/pod-product-compliance
Lightning Source LLC
Chambersburg PA
CBHW042021090426
42811CB00016B/1703